Graphic Novels

by Ashley Rae Harris

Content Consultant
Andrea Wood
Assistant Professor of Media Studies
Winona State University

CORE
LIBRARY

Published by ABDO Publishing Company, PO Box 398166, Minneapolis, MN 55439. Copyright © 2013 by Abdo Consulting Group, Inc. International copyrights reserved in all countries. No part of this book may be reproduced in any form without written permission from the publisher. The Core Library™ is a trademark and logo of ABDO Publishing Company.

Printed in the United States of America,
North Mankato, Minnesota
112012
012013

Editor: Karen Latchana Kenney
Series Designer: Becky Daum

Cataloging-in-Publication Data
Harris, Ashley Rae.
 Graphic novels / Ashley Rae Harris.
   p. cm. -- (Hot topics in media)
Includes index.
ISBN 978-1-61783-733-4
1. Graphic novels--History and criticism--Juvenile literature. 2. Prohibited books--Juvenile literature. I. Title.
741.509--dc14

                                        2012946377

Photo Credits: U.S. Naval Academy/AP Images, cover, 1, 41; Michael Tullberg/Getty Images, 4; Hermann J. Knippertz/AP Images, 7; DC Entertainment/AP Images, 9; Mark Rucker/Transcendental Graphics/Getty Images, 12; Hulton Archive/Getty Images, 15; Marvel Comics/AP Images, 17 (left); Marvel Entertainment/AP Images, 17 (right); Titan Books/AP Images, 18; Bettmann/Corbis/AP Images, 20; Archie Comics/AP Images, 23; AP Images, 25; Matt Sayles/AP Images, 28; Hans Deryk/AP Images, 31; Dan Tuffs/Getty Images, 33; IDW Publishing/AP Images, 36; Evert Elzinga/AP Images, 39, 45

CONTENTS

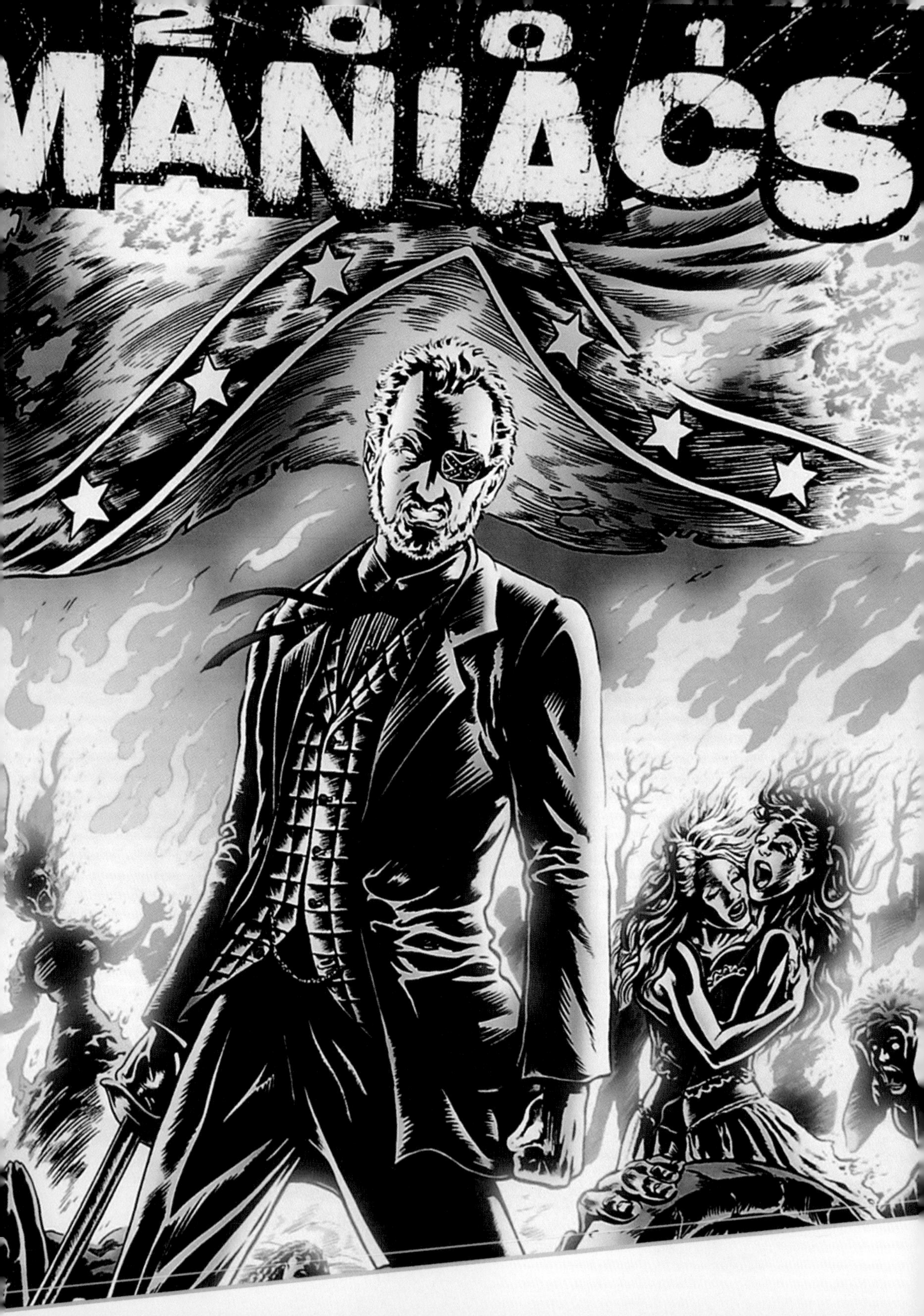
2001
MANIACS™

CHAPTER ONE

From Comic Books to Graphic Novels

I n 1985 it was pretty tough for a kid to buy a comic book. Just a few years before, issues of *The Amazing Spider-Man* could be bought at local newsstands everywhere. But by the mid-1980s, comic books were sold mostly in specialty stores. They seemed to be a dying form of entertainment.

Many graphic novels have dark plots or disturbed characters, such as 2001 Maniacs.

Graphic Novels versus Comic Books

A comic book tells a story through a combination of illustrations and text. Some comic books have almost no words at all. Many comic books are part of a series. Graphic novels can be considered comic books too. But they are typically longer and often have more difficult story lines and themes than comic books. The artwork is often more detailed than in a traditional comic book, and the binding is more durable. Graphic novels are bound like books, while traditional comic books are built more like magazines.

A New Style

But a small group of creative comic book artists were about to publish a new style of comic book. It was longer than a regular comic book. It was meant for a more mature audience. It told a serious or complex story. This new form of comic book became known as the graphic novel and it would forever change the way people thought about comic books.

Spiegelman and *Maus*

One of these graphic novel artists was Art Spiegelman. He was a Jewish immigrant who grew up

Art Spiegelman
in front of an
illustration from
his graphic novel
Maus II

in Queens, New York. Spiegelman got his start in the
comic book world in 1972. He worked for a magazine
published by Marvel Comics. Marvel was one of
the two largest and most important comic book
publishers of all time.

Spiegelman experimented with the genre. He
created a comic book with a personal story. It was
about his father who had survived the Holocaust
during World War II (1939–1945). Spiegelman drew

Jewish characters as mice in the story. Nazi characters were drawn as cats. The story was called *Maus*. It was told in two separate plots. Spiegelman's father is the main character in one plot. He is trying to survive in a concentration camp during the war. The other plot tells the story of Spiegelman's relationship with his father in modern times.

Maus was released as a graphic novel in 1986. Spiegelman received much praise for his unique work. He went on to create a second volume, *Maus II: A Survivor's Tale: And Here My Troubles Began*. The two volumes were combined into one novel. It earned Spiegelman the 1992 Pulitzer Prize, the highest honor in literature.

Graphic Novels of the 1980s

Other artists also published new kinds of comic books. In 1986 Frank Miller and Klaus Janson created *The Dark Knight Returns*. Alan Moore and Dave Gibbons also released *Watchmen* in 1986. The superheroes in these books were not typical.

ONE OF *TIME MAGAZINE'S* 100 BEST NOVELS

WATCHMEN

DC

ALAN MOORE
DAVE GIBBONS

Watchmen is a popular graphic novel series.

Intertextuality in Graphic Novels

One defining element of comic books and graphic novels is that they can be intertextual. They are often part of a series. To understand one book or text, the reader must have read an earlier book or text. For example, readers must be familiar with other *Batman* comics to fully understand *The Dark Knight Returns*.

They were flawed and sad. They sometimes did bad things for the greater good. The books blurred the line between good and evil. They also contained complex stories. They were different from comic books—they were graphic novels.

In an interview for Booksense.com, Christopher Monte Smith asked *Maus* author Art Spiegelman about writing and illustrating comic books. Here is an excerpt from the interview:

> **BookSense.com:** *You've been writing and illustrating comic books since the first flowering of alternative comics in San Francisco in the 1960s. What is it about the art form that satisfies you? Are there things that you can do in a comic book that you can't do in any other art form?*
>
> **Art Spiegelman:** *Comics are a narrative art form, a form that combines two other forms of expression: words and pictures. Like any other medium, it's "value-neutral." There've been lots of rotten novels and paintings, and zillions of rotten comics. But in the hands of someone who knows how to use their medium, great things can happen. Good comics make an impression that lasts forever.*
>
> Source: Spiegelman, Art. "Art Spiegelman: Interview by Christopher Monte Smith."
> IndieBound. *American Booksellers Association, 2008.*
> Web. Accessed November 2, 2012.

What's the Big Idea?

Read Art Spiegelman's answer to the interviewer's questions. What is Spiegelman's main idea? What does he mean when he says that comics are "value-neutral"? What details does he use to support this statement?

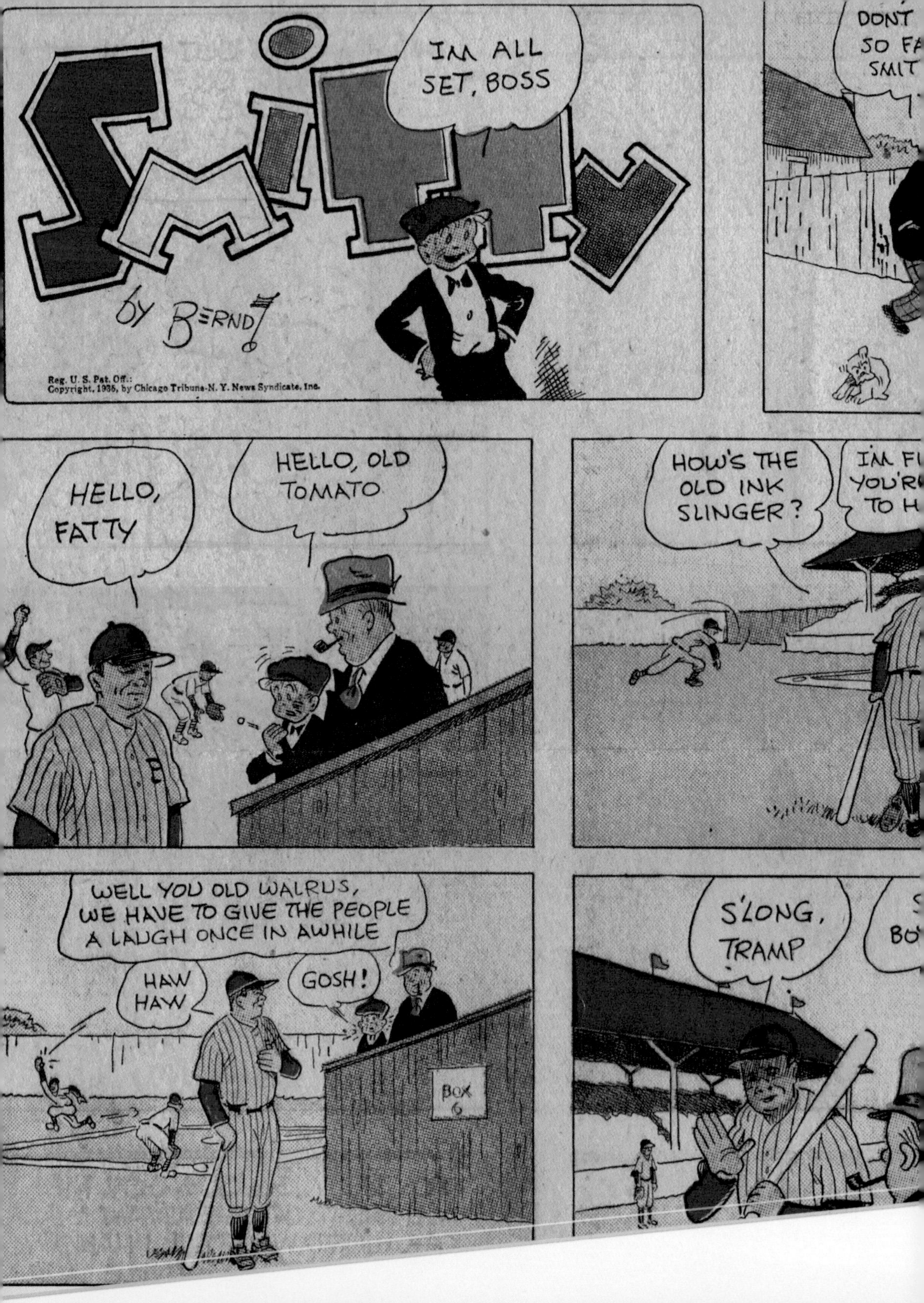
SMITTY
by BERNDT
Reg. U. S. Pat. Off.: Copyright, 1935, by Chicago Tribune-N. Y. News Syndicate, Inc.
IM ALL SET, BOSS
HELLO, FATTY
HELLO, OLD TOMATO
HOW'S THE OLD INK SLINGER?
WELL YOU OLD WALRUS, WE HAVE TO GIVE THE PEOPLE A LAUGH ONCE IN AWHILE
HAW HAW
GOSH!
BOX 6
S'LONG, TRAMP

CHAPTER TWO

How Comic Books Began

Comic strips had been printed in newspapers since the late 1800s. These cartoons typically showed current events or politics in a comic style. In the 1930s publishers began to make books from collections of comic strips. The new comic books flew off the newsstands.

Comic books evolved from newspaper comic strips such as Smitty. The comic strip shown here is from 1935.

DC Comics

Newspaper comic books were popular during the Great Depression (1929–1940s). This was a time when many people and businesses had little or no money. Publishers began making comic books using new comics instead of recycled strips from newspapers.

Harry Donenfeld owned a little printing shop called Donny Press. In 1935 Donenfeld began printing comic books on credit. This meant publishers would pay him for printing after the books sold. He soon became a key player in the comic book business. Donny Press later grew to become Detective Comics (DC Comics).

Donenfeld partnered with Jack Liebowitz to create DC Comics. The company released *Detective Comics* and *Action Comics*. The stories in both centered on fighting crime and solving mysteries. The first issue of *Action Comics* was released in June 1938. It introduced readers to the character Superman, who

Superman became a big hit for DC Comics.

was a hit. Batman was born in the May 1939 issue of *Detective Comics*.

Comics Go Big

Comic books became very popular between 1938 and the mid-1950s. Batman's creators soon created a cast of characters that included the Joker, Robin, and Catwoman. These superheroes dominated the comic book genre.

In 1939 Martin Goodman created Timely Comics, later known. as Marvel Comics. It published a new series called *Marvel Comics*. In this new series two superheroes from separate series were brought together in the same story. These superheroes were

Captain America

Timely Comics' Captain America was one of the most popular superheroes of the World War II era. He was a patriotic hero who symbolized US soldiers fighting against Germany and its allies. His enemy was Red Skull, who represented a German spy.

CAPTAIN AMERICA
MARCH
No. 1
COMICS
45 thrilling pages of CAPTAIN AMERICA
PLUS OTHER GREAT FEATURES!
10¢
SMASHING THRU, CAPTAIN AMERICA CAME FACE TO FACE WITH HITLER...
U.S.A.
also CAPTAIN AMERICA'S YOUNG ALLY, BUCKY
AMERICA
#1
RICK REMENDER
KLAUS JANSON
MARVEL NOW!
JOHN ROMITA
DEAN WHITE
JOIN THE REVOLUTION
001

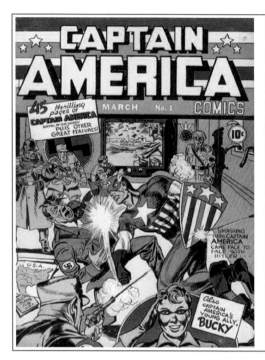

***Captain America*: Then and Now**

The images above show an early Timely Comics' *Captain America* cover next to a 2011 Marvel Comics' *Captain America* cover. Compare these two covers. How are they similar? How are they different? How does the early cover on the left reflect the era (1940s) in which it was created? How might the new cover on the right appeal more to a modern audience?

Human Torch and Namor the Sub-Mariner. They were powerful enemies who fought against each other. Goodman created something new in the world of comics. These connected story lines in different series would become known as the Marvel Universe. Jack Kirby was one of the Marvel Comics artists responsible

Jack Kirby, *left*, and Joe Simon, were the co-creators of the Captain America comic.

FURTHER EVIDENCE

Chapter Two contains information about comic book history. If you could pick out the main point of the chapter, what would it be? What evidence was given to support that point? Visit the Web site below to learn more about the history of comic books. Choose a quote from the Web site that relates to this chapter. Does this quote support the author's main point? Does it make a new point? Write a few sentences explaining how the quote you found relates to this chapter.

Comic Strips

www.kids.britannica.com/comptons/article-198337/cartoons

for creating popular comics such as *Captain America* and *The Incredible Hulk*. Kirby is viewed as one of the most important comic book artists of all time. He made animated cartoons for *Popeye* and *Betty Boop*. Kirby also created romance comics, which were popular with young girl readers.

By 1943 the comic book industry was worth $30 million. *Superman* had its own radio show. The comic book industry was at the top of its game.

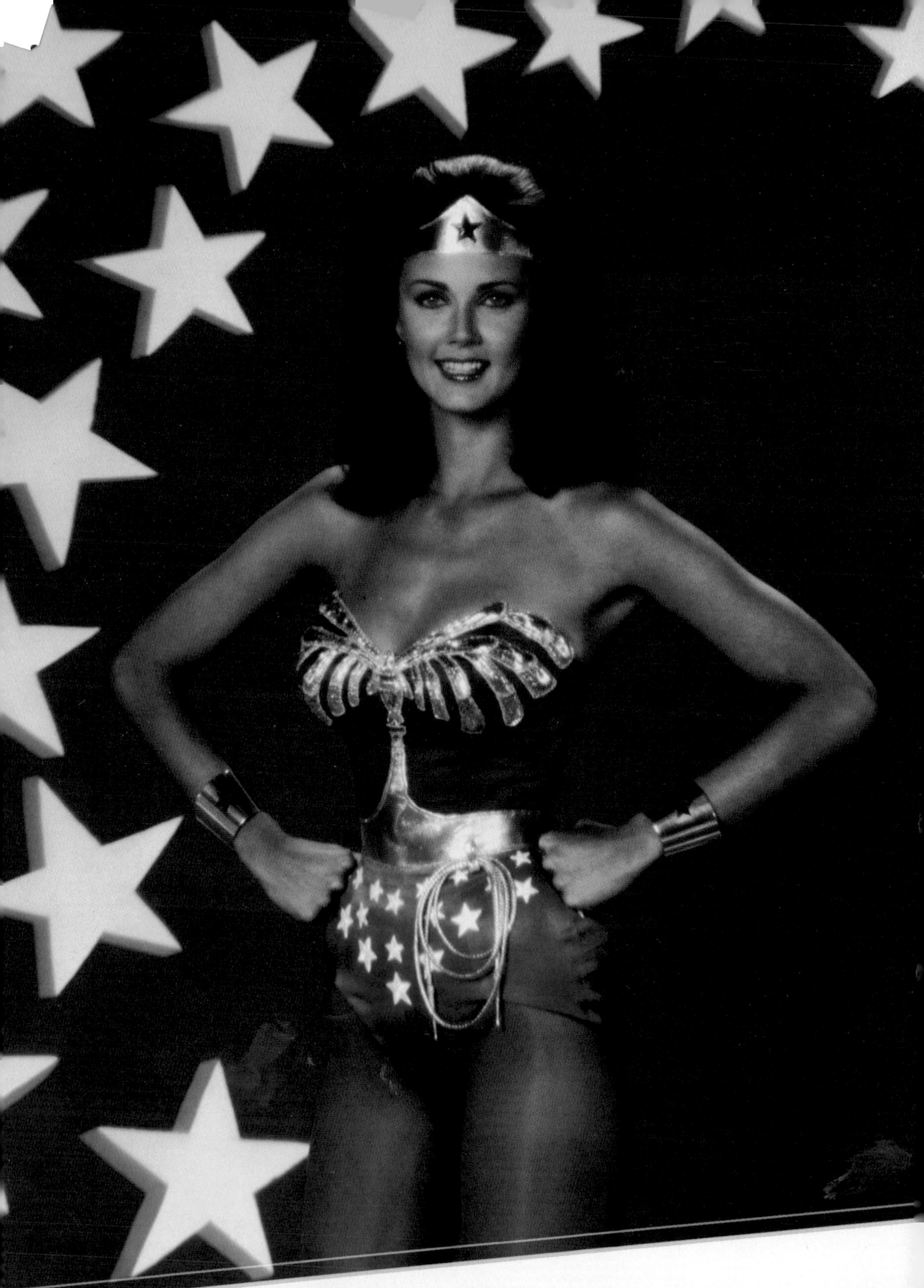

CHAPTER THREE

Comic Books under Fire

In the 1940s comic books went through some changes. Teams of superheroes appeared. Teams had a dominant hero and a supporting group. Each superhero had powers that matched or complemented those of his or her teammates.

Most superheroes were male. But some important female superheroes appeared in the early days. William Molten Marston created *Wonder Woman* in

The first female superhero was Wonder Woman, who was later played by Lynda Carter on a television show about the character.

December 1941. Stories about this famous female superhero are still published today.

Comics and Teenagers

World War II ended in 1945. It resulted in changes to comic book content. Comic books became less focused on war themes. New subjects were funny animals, science fiction, western, jungle, romance, crime and horror, and stories about war veterans. Teens became the main characters in many comics.

Teens had first appeared in comics in 1941. Among the most popular were the series published by Archie Comics. Archie Comics made funny comics

The X-Men

Perhaps the most well-known comic book team of all time is the X-Men. Stan Lee and Jack Kirby created *The X-Men* for Marvel in September 1963. The team consisted of multiple characters who possessed something called the X-gene. It gave them special abilities. Despite the name, *The X-Men* included both male and female superheroes.

A special seventieth anniversary issue of *The Archies* by Archie Comics benefited a charity.

featuring a freckle-faced high school boy named Archie and his friends Jughead, Veronica, and Betty.

A Bad Influence?

Teen characters were often portrayed as innocent and playful in Archie Comics. But the comic book industry soon came under attack for its shift to teen characters. Some people believed the comics were a bad influence on teenagers. In 1954 German psychologist Dr. Fredric Wertham wrote the book *Seduction of the Innocent*. He blamed comic book creators and publishers for many problems with youth, such as failing grades in school.

Some people did not think Wertham's book proved there was anything wrong with comic books. But many people agreed with Wertham. Government officials and the media attacked the comic book industry. Parents complained to stores that sold comic books. Some people even collected comic books to publicly burn them. Some politicians threatened to ban comic books altogether.

Two children add their comic books to the back of a truck for a comic book burning in 1955.

Comics Code of Authority

In an effort to save the industry, publishers and industry insiders formed the Comics Code of Authority (CCA) in 1954. The CCA made a list of rules written by publishers. It had rules against including violence, profanity, and obscenity in comic books.

Each book had to be reviewed by the CCA. The CCA made sure the book was suitable for young readers. Then it received a stamp showing it was cleared by the CCA before going to print. The CCA's rules would be in place until 2011. But they would not always be as strict as they were in the 1950s. The rules were relaxed as time went on. And the rules did not change comic book fans' love for the characters they were reading about.

Gaines and EC Comics

One comic book industry leader refused to sign on to the CCA. This was EC Comics, led by Bill Gaines. EC Comics published *Mad* magazine and *Tales from the Crypt*. When a Senate committee met to discuss comic books, Gaines testified in court against censorship of comic books. After refusing to sign the CCA, Gaines could no longer find places to sell most EC Comics. *Mad* magazine survived because it was a magazine. It did not have to follow the same rules set up by the CCA.

On October 26, 1954, the Comics Magazine Association of America adopted a code that all comic books had to follow in order to be published. Some of the rules were as follows:

(1) Crimes shall never be presented in such a way as to create sympathy for the criminal, to promote distrust of the forces of law and justice, or to inspire others with a desire to imitate criminals.

(2) No comics shall explicitly present the unique details and methods of a crime. . . .

(6) In every instance good shall triumph over evil and the criminal punished for his misdeeds.

Source: "Code of the Comic Books Association of America, Inc."
History Matters. *American Social History Productions, Inc.*, 2012.
Web. Accessed November 2, 2012.

Changing Minds

The text above shows three of the many standards in the CCA. Take a position on one of the standards. Then imagine your best friend has the opposite opinion. Write a short essay trying to change your friend's mind. Make sure you detail your opinion and your reasons for it. Include facts and details that support your reasons.

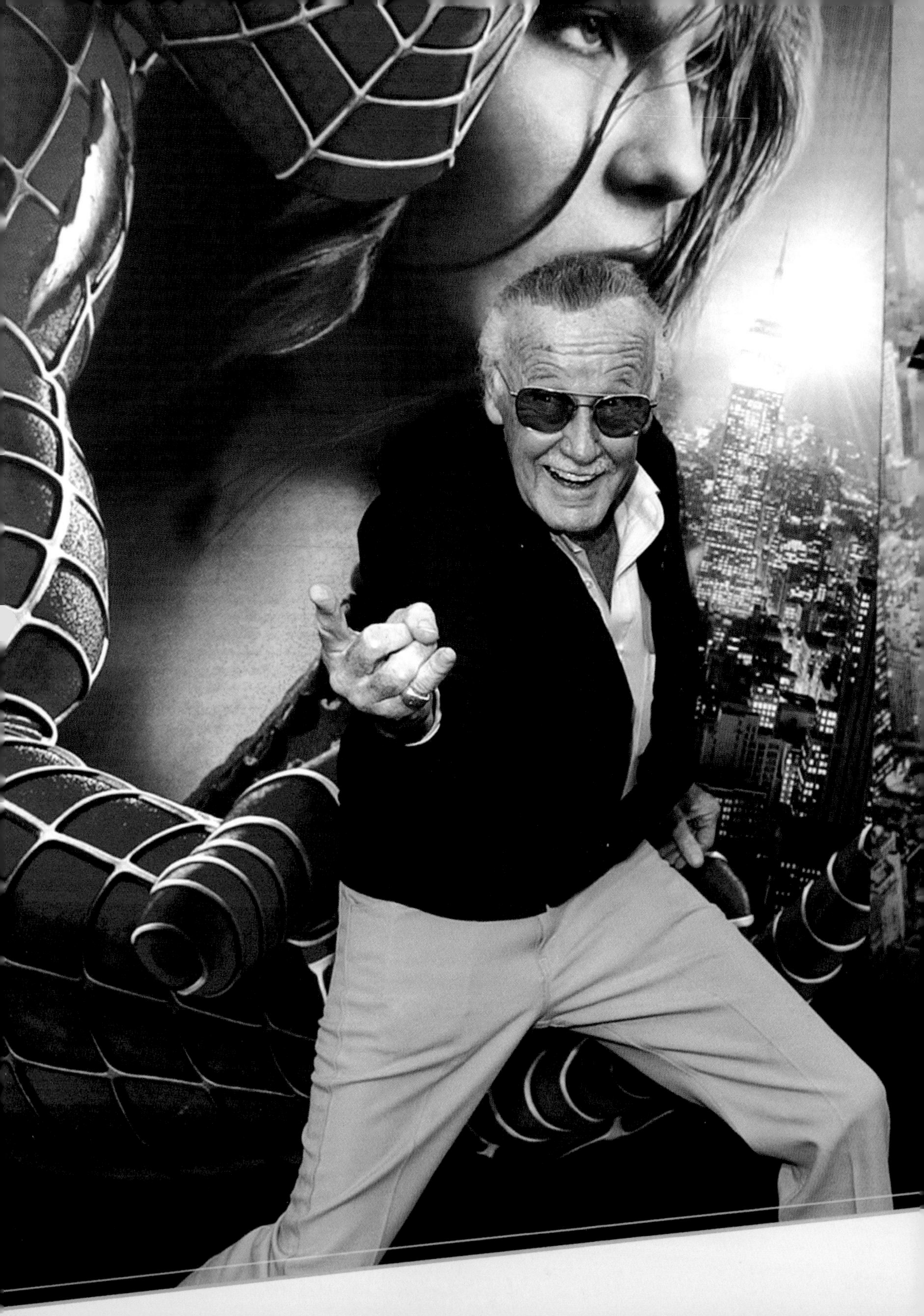

A Fresh Start

The comic book industry returned to the superhero genre throughout the 1960s. In 1961 Stan Lee and Jack Kirby created *The Fantastic Four*. The characters were a family who had acquired superhero powers after being exposed to radiation. *The Fantastic Four* used cliffhanger endings. This meant the books ended in the middle of a dramatic moment. The reader would have to wait until the next

Stan Lee created the comic characters in the Fantastic Four, Spider-Man, and *The Incredible Hulk*.

comic book to find out what happened next. Marvel also launched Stan Lee's *Spider-Man* in August 1962.

Underground Comix

Not all comic books were created by big comic book companies. Some artists produced, printed, and sold books independently. In 1968 artist Robert Crumb's *Zap Comix #1* was sold out of a baby carriage on the streets of San Francisco. Throughout the 1970s a new kind of comics, called *comix*, appeared. These were often produced and printed by independent artists such as Crumb. They did not follow the rules of the CCA. Comix paved the way for mainstream comics to address serious issues and create more diverse characters.

Graphic Novels Emerge

Comic books were not done evolving. Will Eisner changed the genre again when he wrote one of the first graphic novels. His book *A Contract With God* was published in 1978. It examined the lives of

Will Eisner was a pioneer in the graphic novel genre.

Indie Characters

Indie graphic novels were very different from superhero comics. In Daniel Clowes's 2001 *Ghost World*, the main female character is a bored teenage girl living in the suburbs. She uses sarcasm and pranks to entertain herself. Eventually she realizes her bad attitude is only making her lonely. In Craig Thompson's 2003 *Blankets*, the main character is a loner growing up with strict religious parents. He falls in love and begins to question religion for the first time.

immigrants in New York City during the 1930s. Eisner went on to write several more graphic novels. In 1986 more graphic novels were published, including *Watchmen*, *The Dark Knight Returns*, and *Maus*.

The characters in graphic novels had very few of the hero qualities or superhero powers compared to comic book characters of the past. During the 1990s many popular graphic novels featured teenagers with no special powers. These works were called indie graphic novels. The stories focused on characters facing the challenges of growing up.

Daniel Clowes, creator of *Ghost World*, works in his studio in June 2007.

As the graphic novel developed, authors began to address social and political issues. Many graphic novels were very emotional. In 2000 Judd Winick wrote *Pedro and Me: Friendship, Loss and What I Learned*. In his graphic novel, Winick tells the story of a friend who dies of AIDS. Marjane Satrapi wrote *Persepolis: The Story of a Childhood* in 2002. *Persepolis* is Satrapi's true story about growing up as a girl in Iran during a religious revolution.

Manga

Japanese comic books, or *manga*, became popular in the United States in the 1990s. By 2007 manga was the fastest-growing type of graphic novel in the United States.

Changes to Manga

Osamu Tezuka is a well-known manga artist. He changed the Japanese genre in the late 1940s and 1950s. Tezuka was influenced by Disney characters, such as Snow White and Bambi. He created manga characters with huge eyes. His first manga novel was *New Treasure Island*, published in 1947. In 1952 he created *Astro Boy*. It was based on the story of Pinocchio, but the main character was a robot boy.

Manga are very popular with girls and women. Unlike American graphic novels, manga often have teenage girls as leading characters. While some styles focus on themes of love and romance, manga cover a wide range of topics, including historical drama, cooking, and sports.

EXPLORE ONLINE

Chapter Four focuses on different kinds of graphic novels and the artists who created them. The Web site below explains how Will Eisner contributed to the rise of the graphic novel. How is the information given in the Web site different from the information in this chapter? What information is the same? How do the two sources present information differently? What can you learn from this Web site?

Will Eisner Biography: Rise of the Graphic Novel
www.willeisner.com/biography/6-rise-of-the-graphic-novel.html

PRESIDENTIAL MATERIAL:

Barack Obama

CHAPTER FIVE

Graphic Novels in School

Manga is not the only fast-growing graphic novel genre in the United States. Educational graphic novels are also developing quickly. Today teachers find that it is difficult to hold students' attention with traditional textbooks, which contain more text than images. Some have found graphic novels to be a great way

Educational graphic novels, such as this one about President Barack Obama published in 2008, cover all kinds of nonfiction topics.

to appeal to students, particularly in subjects such as history and language studies.

Context and Clues

Pictures help students of different reading and language levels understand content. The pictures provide clues to the meanings of text. They give context to the stories. Graphic novels have been very useful in teaching students who do not speak English as their first language or who are struggling readers. They can help make difficult content easier to understand.

Roots of Educational Graphic Novels

Early comic strips were often used as public service announcements, or PSAs, to raise awareness about health and safety. During World War II, *Spider-Man* creator Stan Lee created posters warning soldiers to avoid infections and diseases while in foreign lands.

The Debate

Many teachers, college professors, and librarians find graphic novels to be very effective learning tools. But graphic novels

A graphic version of *The Diary of Anne Frank* teaches students about the Holocaust.

are not widely accepted as good teaching tools. Some educators worry that students will not develop high-level reading and writing skills when so much content is presented in pictures. Others are concerned they will not be able to teach subject matter through pictures. Despite arguments against them, graphic novels have quickly made their way into the classrooms, backpacks, laptops, and e-book readers of students everywhere.

Bone

The award-winning series *Bone* has been very successful in inspiring students to read. Ohio comic artist Jeff Smith self-published his graphic novel *Bone* in 1991. In nine issues the story of three cousins and their adventures is told. The series is a long, drawn-out saga. It has been compared to ancient epics such as Homer's *The Odyssey*. Teachers sometimes have students read classical mythology alongside *Bone*. This helps students connect graphic novels to other literary forms.

In 2004 the Maryland State Department of Education launched the Maryland Comic Book Initiative to determine how comic books could best be used for teaching and learning. By 2008, 200 schools were participating in the program.

In some ways, educational graphic novels are very different than the comic books that first became available to kids in the 1930s. Graphic novels cover serious topics and are primarily meant for learning—not just entertainment.

Comic books and graphic novels have always been important learning tools. Early comic books

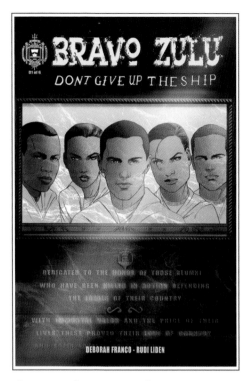

Recruiting with Graphic Novels

In 2009 the US Navy released a graphic novel to interest students in joining the navy. The cover of the novel is shown here. Look closely at it. Why might a graphic novel appeal to students more than a different kind of marketing technique? How do the visual elements of the graphic novel help the creators get their point across?

used superheroes or soldiers to show the difference between right and wrong or power versus weakness. Later comic books helped readers think even more critically about their world. Graphic novels continue to tell serious stories in a new, visual way.

IMPORTANT DATES

1800s

Comic strips are printed in newspapers.

1935

Harry Donenfeld begins printing comic books, and his company later becomes DC Comics.

1938

Action Comics introduces the character of Superman.

1961

Stan Lee and Jack Kirby create The Fantastic Four.

1968

Robert Crumb sells the first underground comix, Zap Comix #1.

1978

Will Eisner's graphic novel A Contract With God is published.

1939

Martin Goodman forms Timely Comics, which later becomes Marvel Comics.

1954

The Seduction of the Innocent by Dr. Frederic Wertham blames comic books for problems with youth.

1954

The Comics Code of Authority is formed.

1986

Maus is released as a graphic novel.

1992

Art Spiegelman wins a Pulitzer Prize for Maus.

2003

Craig Thompson creates the graphic novel Blankets.

STOP AND THINK

Say What?

Studying graphic novels can mean learning a lot of new vocabulary. Find five words in this book you've never seen or heard before. Use a dictionary to find out what they mean. Then write the meanings in your own words, and use each word in a new sentence.

Another View

There are many sources online and in your library about graphic novels. Ask a librarian or other adult to help you find a reliable source on graphic novels. Compare what you learn in this new source with what you have learned in this book. Then write a short essay comparing and contrasting the new source's view of graphic novels to the ideas in this book. How are they different? How are they similar? Why do you think they are different or similar?

Why Do I Care?

This book explains how graphic novels can be used to teach students. List two or three ways you have learned new information from a graphic novel. What did you learn?

Surprise Me

The history and culture of graphic novels can be interesting and surprising. What two or three facts about graphic novels did you find most surprising? Write a few sentences about each fact. Why did you find them surprising?

GLOSSARY

censorship
to ban or cut portions of a book, movie, or other type of media

cliffhanger
an ending of a comic book that leaves the reader in suspense

complex
having many different and connecting parts

genre
a category or style of book or song

Holocaust
the mass murder of Jews under the German Nazi regime from 1941 to 1945

intertextual
the relationship between texts

literature
written works

narrative
a spoken or written account of connected events; a story

sarcasm
the use of irony to mock or show dislike for someone or something

LEARN MORE

Books

Hamilton, Sue L. *Jack Kirby.* Minneapolis: ABDO, 2007.

Hamilton, Sue L. *Stan Lee.* Minneapolis: ABDO, 2007.

Spiegelman, Art. *Maus: A Survivor's Tale.* New York: Pantheon Books, 1986.

Web Links

To learn more about graphic novels, visit ABDO Publishing Company online at **www.abdopublishing.com**. Web sites about graphic novels are featured on our Book Links page. These links are routinely monitored and updated to provide the most current information available.

Visit **www.mycorelibrary.com** for free additional tools for teachers and students.

INDEX

ABOUT THE AUTHOR

Ashley Rae Harris is a graphic novel fan and freelance writer. She has written several books for adolescents. Her work has also appeared in several magazines. She holds a master's degree from the University of Chicago.